How to Pray,
and See God's Answer in the
Clouds Above

How to Pray, and See God's Answer in the Clouds Above

Franklin A. Tyler Jr.

iUniverse, Inc.
New York Lincoln Shanghai

How to Pray, and See God's Answer in the Clouds Above

iUniverse books may be ordered through booksellers or by contacting:

iUniverse
2021 Pine Lake Road, Suite 100
Lincoln, NE 68512
www.iuniverse.com
1-800-Authors (1-800-288-4677)

Because of the dynamic nature of the Internet, any Web addresses or links contained in this book may have changed since publication and may no longer be valid.

ISBN: 978-0-595-47938-2 (pbk)
ISBN: 978-0-595-60018-2 (ebk)

Printed in the United States of America

Dedicated To:

- My beautiful wife Delores Tyler who has always supported me in everything that I do.

- My three children: Angela and her husband Deron; Amy and her husband Johnny; Zachary and his wife San Juana. May they stay happily married for as long as I have been happily married.

- My grandchildren: Delano Hernandez; Johnny Angel Ruiz; Lauryn Edens. Their youthful energy spread to me and gave me the energy and the will power to write this book. May they get their answers to their prayers interpreted from this book.

Contents

Acknowledgements ix

Foreword xi

Introduction xiii

Part I 1

  • *A. How to Pray* *1*

  • *B. Where Should You Pray* *3*

  • *C. Does God Answer Prayer* *4*

  • *D. How God Communicated During Bible Times* *5*

    1. God Talked in Person 5

    2. God Talked in Visions 5

    3. God Talked To People in their Dreams 6

    4. God Talked to People by Writing 6

  • *E. How God Traveled During Old Testament Times* *8*

  • *F. God is Located in Heaven* *10*

Part II 12

  • *A. Today God talks to us from the clouds* *12*

  • *B. A-to-Z Dictionary* *15*

  Words that start with the letter A 15

  Words that start with the letter B 17

  Words that start with the letter C 19

  Words that start with the letter D 22

  Words that start with the letter E 23

  Words that start with the letter F 24

  Words that start with the letter G 25

Words that start with the letter H 26

Words that start with the letter I 27

Words that start with the letter J 28

Words that start with the letter K 29

Words that start with the letter L 30

Words that start with the letter M 31

Words that start with the letter N 32

Words that start with the letter O 33

Words that start with the letter P 34

Words that start with the letter Q 35

Words that start with the letter R 36

Words that start with the letter S 37

Words that start with the letter T 38

Words that start with the letter U 39

Words that start with the letter V 40

Words that start with the letter W 41

Words that start with the letter X 42

Words that start with the letter Y 43

Words that start with the letter Z 44

Endnotes 45

References 49

Acknowledgements

- I want to thank my family for putting up with me all these years. Without their support I would not have written this book.

- I owe a debt of gratitude to Mrs. Pat Strawn, for information she gave me, and for her enthusiastic attitude. This kept me going in the right direction.

- I want to thank Mr. David Salinas, and Mr. Luis Rivera. They gave me hope that my book would succeed when others criticized me. They were the reason that I never lost hope.

- I would like to thank the staff at iUniverse. Without them this book would not have been published.

- I want to thank Rosemary Espinosa Huizar for her technical support.

Foreword

In writing this book I refer to the Holy Bible, and I quote from the Holy Bible. I am well aware that there are different versions of the Holy Bible in circulation today. I am aware that some people prefer one version of the Holy Bible over other versions. For this book I use "The World English Bible" (WEB). I use this version of the Holy Bible because it a Public Domain no copyright, and anyone has access to it, and may reproduce, and share it with others without permission, and without having to pay a fee. This Holy Bible is on the internet and may be found at http://eBible.org/web/. This version of the Holy Bible is a modern English translation of the Holy Bible. It is based on the American Standard Version of the Holy Bible.

If you are worried that "The World English Bible" is not translated the way "your" Holy Bible is, all that you need to do is go to the Scripture line and verse in "your" Holy Bible, that I refer to in my book, and see what your Bible says. I'm sure you will find that it has the same meaning as the WEB Bible. Beware not to get wrapped up in the controversy about what Holy Bible is the correct one to use.

Introduction

Have you ever wondered if God answers your prayers? Or have you wondered if you are praying the "right way"? You are not alone. People all over the world have these thoughts, and have had these thoughts for thousands of years. Many people have never found out, and many people will never find out the answer to these questions. But, you can with the information in this book. This book will explain to you the proper way to pray, and the right way to see God's answers to your prayers. I have done extensive research into prayer and how God answers prayers. The Bible that I use for my reference material is "The World English Bible" (WEB). I will go over certain Bible verses with you concerning these topics, and what these verses mean. I will also go over several Bible verses that show that God travels on clouds, and that He can be heard from clouds. I will also make the connection that we can see God's answers to our prayers in the clouds above. I have interviewed hundreds of people from the United States, as well as foreign countries since 1982. I was able to do this because I was in the United States Army from December 1971 through December 1991, and I was stationed in Germany three times as well as several States in the United States. I was able to travel in Germany, Switzerland, Italy, and France. I was able to interview people where I was stationed who have seen the answers to their prayers in the clouds. I have compiled a list of their problems, how they prayed, and then the different clouds that they saw, and what the meanings of the clouds were. I have included an A-to-Z dictionary on what those hundreds of people saw in the clouds, and what they meant to them so that you can apply them to help you interpret God's answers to your prayers.

Here is one eyewitness account of a person seeing the answer to his prayer in the clouds above. I interviewed Mr. Salinas in San Antonio Texas. This is what he told me. "I was driving my car on the highway, with my son in the back seat. We were going to the store. I glanced up at the sky and saw several cumulus clouds. I looked back at the road and continued driving. My son yelled at me from the back seat 'look at the clouds Dad!' and I instantly looked up at the sky. What I saw amazed me. I saw a cumulus cloud in the shape of a capital letter D. It was clearly a D, and my son pointed it out because my first name is David, and of course my son knew that. I wondered what was going on. Was this a message for me? Or was it a coincidence? I kept my eyes on the road and continued driving a few more minutes, when all of a sudden my son yells out again 'look at the sky Dad!' and I looked up at the sky and saw that the cumulus cloud that had turned into the letter D was now a symbol of a fish, the kind Christians put on the back of their cars, and they stick by magnet or glue. I talked about this sighting with my son. I told him that I believe that God gave me a personal message by showing me the letter D to get my attention, then the symbol of a fish to get me to turn back to God."[1]

Part I

A. HOW TO PRAY

In the New Testament of the Bible according to Luke one of Jesus' disciples inquired of Jesus how they should pray. Luke 11:1 says: "It happened, that when he finished praying in a certain place, one of his disciples said to him, 'Lord, teach us to pray, just as John also taught his disciples'."[2]

You are not alone in asking how to pray. Here we have disciples asking Jesus how to pray.

In the New testament of the Bible, according to Matthew 6:9-13 the Bible verse says: "Pray like this: 'Our Father in heaven, may your name be kept holy. Let your Kingdom come. Let your will be done, as in heaven, so on earth. Give us today our daily bread. Forgive us our debts, as we also forgive our debtors. Bring us not into temptation, but deliver us from the evil one. For yours is the Kingdom, the power, and the glory forever. Amen.'"[3]

Luke 11:2-4 Says: "He said to them, 'When you pray, say, Our Father in heaven, may your name be kept holy. May your Kingdom come. May your will be done on earth, as it is in heaven. Give us day by day our daily bread. Forgive us our sins, for we ourselves also forgive everyone who is indebted to us. Bring us not into temptation, but deliver us from the evil one.'"[4]

So you see from the verses above that this is supposed to be a model for our prayer. This is known as "The Lord's Prayer." It begins with adoration of God, acknowledges subjection to His will, asks petitions of Him, and ends with praise. Does this mean this is the only way to pray? I don't believe so. I believe this should be the start of your prayer and then just talk to God like you would talk to a person. I believe that you just have to follow this format. If you don't pray in this manner, will God still listen to your prayer? I believe that God will still listen to your prayer. This gives a person that does not have any idea how to pray an example how to pray.

2 Chronicles 7:14 says: "if my people, who are called by my name, shall humble themselves, and pray, and seek my face, and turn from their wicked ways; then I will hear from heaven, and will forgive their sin, and will heal their land."[5]

Here we have God telling everyone what to do when they pray, to get blessings. Let's look closer at the passage "seek my face" in the passage above. I believe that tells us to actually see the image of his face by looking in the clouds above.

B. WHERE SHOULD YOU PRAY

According to Matthew 6:5-8: "When you pray, you shall not be as the hypocrites, for they love to stand and pray in the synagogues and in the corners of the streets, that they may be seen by men. Most certainly, I tell you, they have received their reward. But you, when you pray, enter into your inner room, and having shut your door, pray to your Father who is in secret, and your Father who sees in secret will reward you openly. In praying, don't use vain repetitions, as the Gentiles do; for they think that they will be heard for their much speaking. Therefore don't be like them, for your Father knows what things you need, before you ask him."[6]

This means that you should pray without making it a big deal. You should not be a show off when you pray. Some translations of the Bible tell you to go into a closet to pray. I believe that this passage is not telling you to literally go in a closet to pray, but it means that you can pray anywhere and keep it low key.

C. DOES GOD ANSWER PRAYER

Luke 11:9-13 says: "I tell you, keep asking, and it will be given you. Keep seeking, and you will find it. Keep knocking, and it will be opened to you. For everyone who asks receives. He who seeks find. To him that knocks it will be opened. Which of you fathers, if your son asks for bread, will give him a stone? Or if he asks for a fish, he won't give him a snake instead of a fish, will he? Or if he asks for an egg, he won't give him a scorpion, will he? If you then, being evil, know how to give good gifts to your children, how much more will your heavenly Father give the Holy Spirit to those who ask him?"[7]

The above passage means that God will answer your prayers and give you what you ask for.

Should you expect an answer to your prayer right away, or will the answer take some time? When you get the answer will you recognize it as the answer? Will the answer come as a voice, a face, a dream, a vision, writing, or will the answer come in a cloud? Will you get the answer in actions or signs? To find out the answers to these questions let's continue to the next chapter.

D. How God Communicated During Bible Times

1. God Talked in Person

The first and second time that the Bible mentions God talking is in Genesis 1:3: "God said, 'Let there be light': and there was light."[8] And in Genesis 1:6: "God said, 'Let there be an expanse in the middle of the waters, and let it divide the waters from the waters.'"[9]

We can see from these passages that God talked. Here he was not talking to anyone in particular, he was just talking out loud.

When God created the world God talks to no one in particular, and when He created Adam and Eve God talked to them. In Genesis 1:28 "… God said to them, 'Be fruitful, multiply, fill the earth, and subdue it. Have dominion over the fish of the sea, over the birds of the sky, and over every living thing that moves on the earth.'"[10]

We can see from these passages that God did talk in person to people during Bible times.

2. God Talked in Visions

In Genesis 15:1: "After these things the word of Yahweh came to Abram in a vision, saying, 'Don't be afraid, Abram. I am your shield, your exceedingly great reward.'"[11]

So here we see that God came in a vision and talked to Abram.

In Genesis 15:2: "Abram said, 'Lord Yahweh, what will you give me, since I go childless, and he who will inherit my estate is Eliezer of Damascus?'"[12]

Here we see that in Abrams vision of God talking to him, Abram talks to God as if he has conversations with other people.

In Numbers 12:5-6: "Yahweh came down in the pillar of cloud, and stood at the door of the Tent, and called Aaron and Miriam; and they both came forward. He said, 'Hear now my words. If there is a prophet among you, I Yahweh will make myself known to him in a vision. I will speak with him in a dream.'"[13]

So we can see that God talked to people in visions during Bible times.

3. God Talked To People in their Dreams

In Genesis 28:12-16: "He dreamed. Behold, a stairway set upon the earth, and its top reached to heaven. Behold, the angels of God ascending and descending on it. Behold, Yahweh stood above it, and said, 'I am Yahweh, God of Abraham your father, and the God of Isaac. The land whereon you lie, to you will I give it, and to your seed. Your seed will be as the dust of the earth, and you will spread abroad to the west, and to the east, and to the north, and to the south. In you and in your seed will all the families of the earth be blessed. Behold, I am with you, and will keep you, wherever you go, and will bring you again into this land. For I will not leave you, until I have done that which I have spoken of to you'. Jacob awakened out of his sleep, and he said, 'Surely Yahweh is in this place, and I didn't know it.'"[14]

Here we see that God talked to Jacob while Jacob was dreaming. It was a conversation like people would have conversations today. So we can see that God talked to people in visions during Bible Times.

4. God Talked to People by Writing

In Exodus 24:12: "Yahweh said to Moses, 'Come up to me on the mountain, and stay here, and I will give you the tables of stone with the law and commands that I have written, that you may teach them.'"[15]

Here we have God telling Moses to meet him on the Mount so God can give him tablets that God wrote.

Exodus 31:18: "He gave to Moses, when he finished speaking with him on Mount Sinai, the two tablets of the testimony, stone tablets, written with the God's finger."[16]

Here again we see that God has written on stone tablets.

Deuteronomy 9:10: "Yahweh delivered to me the two tables of stone written with the finger of God; and on them were all the words which Yahweh spoke with you on the mountain out of the midst of the fire in the day of the assembly."[17]

Here again we see that God wrote on the tablets.

Daniel 5:1: "Belshazzar the king made a great feast to a thousand of his lords, and drank wine before the thousand."[18]

Daniel 5:5: "In the same hour came forth fingers of a man's hand, and wrote over against the lampstand on the plaster of the wall of the king's palace: and the king saw the part of the hand that wrote."[19]

Daniel 5:25: "This is the writing that was inscribed, MENE, MENE, TEKEL, UPHARSIN."[20]

Daniel 5:26: "This is the interpretation of the thing: MENE; God has numbered your kingdom, and brought it to an end;"[21]

Daniel 5:27: "TEKEL; Thou are weighed in the balances, and are found wanting."[22]

Daniel 5:28: "PERES; your kingdom is divided, and given to the Medes and Persians."[23]

Daniel 5:30: "In that night Belshazzar the Chaldean King was slain."[24]

Here we see that God wrote on a wall during Bible times.

E. HOW GOD TRAVELED DURING OLD TESTAMENT TIMES

According to Exodus 13:21-22: "Yahweh went before them by day in a pillar of cloud, to lead them on their way, and by night in a pillar of fire, to give them light, that they may go by day and by night: the pillar of cloud by day, and the pillar of fire by night, didn't depart from the people."[25]

This means that God was in the sky in a "pillar of cloud," above the people, leading and protecting them.

Here is another example of the Lord/Cloud connection: In Exodus 16:10: "It happened, as Aaron spoke to the whole congregation of the children of Israel that they looked toward the wilderness, and behold, the glory of Yahweh appeared in the cloud."[26]

This means the people saw the Lord in a cloud.

Here is another example of the Lord/Cloud connection: In Exodus 19:9: "Yahweh said to Moses, 'Behold, I come to you in a thick cloud, that the people may hear when I speak with you, and may also believe you forever.' Moses told the words of the people to the Lord."[27]

This passage tells us that God wants the people to hear him. God talks to Moses from within a thick cloud.

Here is another example of the Lord/Cloud connection: In Numbers 11:25: "Yahweh came down in the cloud, and spoke to him, and took of the Spirit that was on him, and put it on the seventy elders: and it happened, that when the Spirit rested on them, they prophesied, but they did so no more."[28]

This passage tells us that God traveled on a cloud.

Here is another example of the Lord/Cloud connection: In Isaiah 19:1: "The burden of Egypt: 'Behold, Yahweh rides on a swift cloud, and comes to Egypt. The idols of Egypt will tremble his presence; and the heart of Egypt will melt in its midst.'"[29]

This passage tells us that God travels on a swift cloud.

And finally, here is another example of the Lord/Cloud connection. In Matthew 17:5: "While he was still speaking, behold, a bright cloud overshadowed them. Behold, a voice came out of the cloud, saying, 'This is my beloved Son, in whom I am well pleased. Listen to him.'"[30]

This passage tells us that God speaks from within a bright cloud.

From the passages above you can see that God was in a pillar of a cloud in the sky. God appeared to the people in a cloud. God appeared to the people in a thick cloud, they could not see him, but they could see the thick cloud, and they could hear him, God came down to Earth on a cloud, God rode on a swift cloud, God was in a bright cloud, they could not see him but they could hear him talk to them from within the cloud. You can see from the above passages that clouds play an important part when dealing with God.

F. GOD IS LOCATED IN HEAVEN

When you have a conversation with someone you usually know where they are located, or where they are calling from. Well this holds true with praying or talking to God. You want to know where God is talking to you from. To answer this question we must search the Bible, and we will find that God lives in Heaven, and talks to us from Heaven. So now we have two more questions to ask: What is Heaven? Where is Heaven?

Let's search the Bible to find the answers to these questions. I will show you Bible verses on where God talks to us from, where Heaven is, and what Heaven is.

In Genesis 1:1: "In the beginning God created the heavens and the earth."[31]

This passage tells us that God created Heaven when he created the Earth.

In Genesis 1:14-18: "'Let there be lights in the expanse of the sky to divide the day from the night; and let them be for signs, and for seasons, and for days, and years; and let them be for lights in the expanse of the sky to give light on the earth;' and it was so. God made two great lights: the greater light to rule the day, and the lesser light to rule the night. He also made the stars. God set them in the expanse of sky to give light to the earth, and to rule over the day and over the night, and to divide the light from the darkness. God saw that it was good."[32]

We can see from these passages that God created, and placed the Sun, Moon, and the Stars in Heaven, to light the Earth. So then Man could tell the difference in the seasons, by looking into Heaven at the Sun, the Moon, and the Stars. Man could tell days and years also. If we look up at the sky today, we can see the Sun, the Moon, and the Stars. These are the same ones that God created in Genesis.

In Deuteronomy 4:39: "Know therefore this day, and lay it to your heart, that Yahweh he is God in heaven above, and on the earth beneath; there is none else."[33]

This passage shows us that God is in Heaven, and that Heaven is above Earth.

In Deuteronomy 26:15: "Look down from your holy habitation, from heaven, and bless your people Israel, and the ground which you have given us, as you swore to our fathers, a land flowing with milk and honey."[34]

This passage has a person speaking (Moses) to God. The speaker is stating that God is in Heaven, his habitation, which means God's place of residence. This passage also asks God to look down at Israel. This means that Heaven is above Earth.

In Psalms 33:13: "Yahweh looks from heaven. He sees all the sons of men."[35]

This passage tells us that God is in Heaven, and looking at all of us.

In Psalms 102:19: "For he has looked down from the height of his sanctuary. From heaven, Yahweh saw the earth;"[36]

This passage tells us God is in Heaven high above the Earth.

In Psalms 147:8: "who covers the sky with clouds, who prepares rain for the earth, who makes grass grow on the mountains."[37]

This passage tells us that God has many clouds in Heaven above.

In Mark 11:25: "When ever you stand praying, forgive, if you have anything against anyone; so that your Father, who is in heaven, may also forgive you your transgressions."[38]

This passage tells us that God is in heaven.

In Mark 14:62: "Jesus said, 'I am. You will see the Son of Man sitting at the right hand of Power, and coming with the clouds of the sky.'"[39]

This passage tells us God is in Heaven, and will come from the clouds that are in Heaven.

In John 6:38: "For I came down from heaven, not to do my own will, but the will of him who sent me."[40]

This passage tells us that Jesus came down to Earth from Heaven above to do God's will.

So we have seen from the above passages that God "lives" in Heaven. That Heaven is above the earth, and that the Sun, Moon, Stars, and Clouds, are in Heaven.

Part II

A. TODAY GOD TALKS TO US FROM THE CLOUDS

Before I explain how God talks to us using the clouds, let me show you a bible verse that tells us how God <u>doesn't</u> want us to try to talk to Him, or reach Him, or get signs from Him: by making children pass through fire; by divination; by observer of times; by an enchanter; by a witch; by a charmer; by a consulter of familiar spirits; by a wizard; by a necromancer. We can read this in Deuteronomy 18:9-12: "When you have come into the land which Yahweh your God gives you, you shall not learn to do after the abominations of those nations. There shall not be found with you anyone who makes his son or his daughter to pass through the fire, one who uses divination, one who practices sorcery, or an enchanter, or a sorcerer, or a charmer, or a consulter with a familiar spirit, or a wizard, or a necromancer. For whoever does these things is an abomination to Yahweh: and because of these abominations Yahweh your God does drive them out before you."[41]

God does not tell us anywhere in the Bible that we cannot pray to him and see his answer to our prayer in the clouds above.

God has not talked to humans for thousands of years by talking in person; talking in visions; talking in dreams; writing on walls. There must be another way that God is communicating with humans today. I believe that God has shown us in the past how important clouds are when it comes to dealing with him. I believe that God "talks" to humans through clouds today. He gives us "signs" in the clouds. He gives us the answers to our prayers in the clouds.

I have been doing research into this subject since 1982. I wanted to know how God "talked" to people. So I studied the Bible, listened to the radio, watched television, read books, read magazines, and went to several different denomination churches, and I asked a lot of questions. Sometimes I would hear the preachers say that God talked to them and told them what to preach. Sometimes the preachers would say that God talked to them by giving them "signs". Sometimes

I would hear the preachers say that God talked to them by giving them a "feeling" or sixth sense. No one could prove any of this. You were just supposed to take their word for it. They would say that if you didn't believe them, that you didn't have the Holy Spirit. So I continued searching. Several years passed.

Then one day I prayed to God and asked him if he still talked to humans. I asked him to show me a sign that I could understand that it was from Him. Several hours later I took my wife to a doctor's appointment. My grandson Delano Tyler Hernandez was with us. Delano and I stayed in the car, while my wife went to her appointment. I read a newspaper in the front seat of the car, and Delano played an electronic video game in the back seat of the car. While I was reading my newspaper a shadow came across the pages of my newspaper, and darkened it. I put the newspaper down and looked up at the sky. There were several clouds in the sky, and one of the clouds had covered the sun's rays. That's what darkened my newspaper. I started thinking about how God talks to humans, and I prayed for God to give me a sign now, to show me how God talks to humans. I looked at the cloud for several minutes. Then I saw the face of Jesus. I knew it was the face of Jesus by the drawings and pictures I have seen that are supposed to portray Jesus. The sun was behind the face of Jesus, and the sun's rays were shining through His eyes. I thanked God for my answer. I told Delano to stop playing his game and put it down. He did. Then I asked him to look up into the sky and tell me what he saw. He looked up, and around, and then he told me that he saw Jesus in the clouds. He pointed at the same cloud I had looked at, and he too saw the face of Jesus. My wife came out of her appointment, and as we drove home I told her about the face of Jesus. When we got home, I had Delano draw a picture of what he saw. He did.

Over the years I have interviewed hundreds of people from the United States, and foreign countries who have prayed to God and then gotten their answer to their prayer by looking skyward into the clouds. I have compiled a list of their questions, and then I compiled a list of the "signs" they saw in the clouds to see what the meaning to the "signs" were. I do not believe that I have every question, and answer from God to all prayers. I do believe that God has shown me, that the answer to people's prayers can be seen in the clouds above. I am not claiming that God told me to look in the clouds for answers. I am saying that based on the information I have, and the research that I have done, I came to the conclusion that we can see God's answer to our prayers in the clouds.

I believe that today more than ever God gives us messages that are in the clouds that most of us ignore. I also believe that God answers all prayers, and quickly. Sometimes the answer is not the one we want, so we ignore it, sometimes the answer is given and we don't recognize it as the answer. I believe God gives the answers in the clouds above us. The answers come to us in the shapes of the clouds. Let me give you an example: If you pray to God and make a request from him, go outdoors and look in the sky. Ask God to show you his will or the answer to your question. If there is a group of cumulus clouds (puffy clouds) in the sky, or just one cloud, gaze at the clouds for up to 15 minutes. If you see the letter A in the clouds, go to the A-to-Z Dictionary portion of this book and look up what it means. After you look it up, and see the meaning, you need to use this as a guide to either make changes in your life or accept the consequences. If there are no clouds in the sky, you must come back at a latter time. When you are gazing at the clouds in the sky sit down, or lie down, and make yourself comfortable. God will give you a sign that he heard your request, and he will give you a sign on what the answer to your request is. The sign he will give you will be in the clouds. If you gaze at a cloud, or cloud formation for a period of time, you will see that the clouds change shape. So if you are waiting for a sign from God make sure you don't look away from the clouds or you may miss the sign because of the clouds changing shapes. When the cloud or clouds take a shape that is in my A-to-Z Cloud dictionary you have your answer. If the cloud changes shape again, and you have not prayed to God again for an answer to a new question use the first shape as your answer. You can ask complex questions and/or yes and no questions. You can ask any question you want to. If there are a lot of clouds in the sky and you can't figure out what cloud has your message look at airplanes, or birds flying overhead. Where they cross a certain cloud, this will be the cloud that has your answer. The message you see in the clouds could be outlined by the clouds, so the blue sky can be seen as the message. The message could be two or more clouds making up the message. The message could be right side up, the normal way or it could be inverted, inside out and/or backwards. I recommend you take a picture of the message so that you can look at the cloud at all angles to see your message.

Clouds in the sky can be a picture show for you. All you have to do is look. Most people glance at the sky and see the clouds, but they don't stare at the clouds long enough to see the messages that are in the clouds. God has been giving us answers to their prayers for thousands of years. Most of us have not paid attention to them. Now that you know where to look, and how to look, there is no excuse for not looking and receiving God's answer to your prayers.

B. A-to-Z Dictionary

The following is an A-to-Z Dictionary. This will help guide you in understanding Gods answers to your prayers. This is not an all inclusive dictionary but it covers many of the answers that are common to most people.

A

The letter A: To see the Letter A in the clouds stands for several things. It is the first letter of a name, place, or thing.

Ace: To see an Ace in the clouds reveals that you will be selected as number one in a business, in a game, or in taking a test. You will have to work and study hard but you will accomplish your goal.

Acorn: To see an acorn in the clouds points out that you are going to be successful in any area that you strive for. You have to do is build a proper foundation before your efforts will produce favorable results.

Airplane: To see an airplane in the clouds shows that you will get news from a person who lives far away and/or you will be able to travel soon.

Aliens: To see an alien in the clouds points out that there are strangers coming into your life that you need to beware of. If you are seeking a companion, this is not the one. Keep looking.

Alligator: To see an alligator in the clouds reveals a warning to you that someone is going to try to fool you. This person is a low life and lives on the bad side of town.

Anchor: To see an anchor in the clouds warns that you need to budget yourself, or you will find yourself out of funds.

Angel: To see an Angel in the clouds is a clear sign that you are being protected, and you will succeed in your business. Remember that there are good, and bad Angels, so you need to make sure you are following God's will, and not the Devil's will.

Animal: See Cat, Dog Etc.

Anteater: To see an anteater in the clouds reveals there may be a financial dilemma coming your way. It shows that you will have a hard time finding food or buying food.

Antelope: To see an antelope in the clouds reveals that your finances will increase. It indicates that you will have to travel to get this success.

Antenna: To see an antenna in the clouds shows your ability to interpret what is being said to you, and this improves your chances of getting extra profits. You must listen to inner self on this issue.

Anvil: To see an anvil in the clouds is a sign that you are going to be very lucky, but you will have to spend a lot of money, and time before you get a pay-out. You are capable of doing anything as long as you have support from your family.

Ape: To see an ape in the clouds points out that there is a person that you are associated with who is very mischievous. This person will cause you a lot of problems. You need to stay away from this person.

Apple: To see an apple in the clouds shows you will get your just rewards for doing a good job. Your ability to control your emotions will continue to improve. You have done the right things so now all you have to do is wait for it to pay off.

Ark: To see an ark in the clouds is a clear sign that things are favorable for you and good things are coming your way. The item you are looking for is in a small chest or box.

Arm: To see an arm in the clouds is a sign that there are good times ahead, and you have the ability to reach out and help someone. This also means that you need to make sure you arm yourself in your home to safeguard yourself and your family.

Armadillo: To see an armadillo in the clouds points out that you are not outgoing enough, and don't want to share your feelings with others. It is time to open up. You need to move out and about in the daytime not just the nighttime.

Arrow: To see an arrow in the clouds reveals that someone that is close to you that you trust, should not be trusted. It also shows you the direction that you need to travel.

Asp: See Snakes.

Ass: See Donkey.

Astronaut: To see an astronaut in the clouds shows that you need to get a grasp on the big picture. Don't just use the information you have in front of you. You need to research to find the answer you seek. The answer is not a simple one to find.

Automobile: See Car, Truck, or Motorcycle.

Ax: To see an ax in the clouds is a sign that you have done a good job, and you will get your just reward. But you will have to do hard work, and have the right tools in order for this to happen.

B

The letter B: To see the letter B in the clouds stands for a name, of a person, place, or thing. If your prayer was about a certain color, this means it could be the color black, blue, or brown.

Baby: To see a baby in the clouds points out that your friends are going to help you and you will have a new beginning that leads to success. You are considered a person in the group that others like to look out for.

Ballerina: To see a ballerina in the clouds reveals that you are succeeding in life with little problem and you will continue to have success. You move through life with grace, and others would like to emulate you.

Balloon: To see a balloon in the clouds shows that you will have a minor setback but you will bounce back. In the future do not buy anything that has a lump sum payment at the end of the term.

Banana: To see a banana in the clouds is a sign that you will be lucky in a small matter, and you will get small rewards from job performance. You need to eat a better diet that includes fruit.

Basketball: You have been working yourself too hard, and it is time to take a break. You need to get out and play a sport.

Bat: To see a bat (flying mammal) in the clouds points out that you need to beware. A person in your life will turn out to be a back stabber. You need to be careful what you say when they are around. Insects are causing you problems at your home. You need to take care of this problem or it will get worse. To see a bat (a club used to strike a ball in baseball) in the clouds points out that you need to use the proper tool for the job. If you don't use the proper tool you will get a setback.

Bear: To see a bear in the clouds reveals that you will have enough strength to overcome all obstacles that are placed in front of you. You will be called on to take on a bigger burden. You can do it.

Beaver: To see a beaver in the clouds shows that with hard work and perseverance you will achieve your goals. You are a self starter at work and you should continue to give advice.

Bed: To see a bed in the clouds is a sign that you will have job security. This also points out that you will entertain visitors. Make sure you have a proper foundation or the bed may come crashing down.

Bird: To see a bird in the clouds shows that you are on the right track and will be very happy very soon. You need to keep on your diet for better health.

Boar: To see a boar in the clouds reveals that you will have some disappointments over a course of time. You need to dig in and work smarter not harder.

Boat: To see a boat in the clouds shows that you can be in control of your life. Take charge and don't take no for an answer. Once you set a course stay on it.

Body: To see a body in the clouds is a sign that you will have success in what ever you do. Start now even if you can't see the finish line.

Bone: To see a bone in the clouds is a sign that you are in for an inheritance, and it also means that you should get a medical check up. You need to get more information from your doctor.

Boy: To see a boy in the clouds points to your good fortune and playful nature. You need to stop using racial terms or you could be in for trouble.

Brain: To see a brain in the clouds reveals that you need to show more compassion toward your relatives and not be so sarcastic. It also shows that people look up to you for guidance.

Buffalo: To see a buffalo in the clouds shows that you are due to get money from an unlikely source. You need to find easier ways to do things. Work smarter not harder.

Bull: To see a bull in the clouds is a sign that you will have a great and prosperous lifestyle as long as you show initiative. There is someone who is trying to get you to do what they want. Stick to your plan, and don't give in to their requests.

C

The letter C: To see the letter C in the clouds stands for a name of a person, place, or thing. You will know which it is by the people you know. If not ask your family for help.

Calf: To a see a calf in the clouds points out that you are going to realize all that you hoped and worked for. A younger person who is close to you is going to get into trouble, and not tell you all the details.

Camel: To see a camel in the clouds reveals that you will have to work hard so that you can prosper beyond imagination. To prosper you need to prepare in advance. You have the stamina to finish the task you set out to do. Don't let anything stop you.

Candy: To see a piece of candy in the clouds shows that you are soon going to be the happiest you have been in a long time. Don't give up hope. Do not over indulge in any type of food.

Cannon: To see cannon in the clouds is a sign that you will achieve great things. You will have to make minor changes in what you're doing. You need to make sure that you have the proper equipment to do the job.

Canoe: To see a canoe in the clouds points out that you are in full control of your life. You have the ability to navigate to your destination. You need to be careful that you don't rock the boat.

Cap: To see a cap in the clouds reveals an end to your problems after a short amount of time. You should wear a cap when working outside in the sun.

Car: To see a car in the clouds is a sign that you are on the right track. You are in control of your life. Keep going in the direction that you're going. Make sure you have enough gasoline in the car to get were your going.

Cat: To see a cat in the clouds shows you are surrounded by people that are fooling you so that they can get ahead at your expense. You need to research anything they tell you to make sure you are doing the correct thing. You need to check with your supervisor before you do anything they tell you.

Catcher's mitt: To see a catcher's mitt in the clouds is a sign that you are taking on too much responsibility. You need to back up and regroup.

Chain: To see a chain in the clouds points out you have been suffering for too long. Get out of the rut you're in. Seek help from a close friend.

Chair: To see a chair in the clouds reveals some unexpected news coming soon. You need to relax and wait for the news. You will be placed in charge of an important project.

Child: To see a child in the clouds shows that you will prosper in the future, by thinking back to your younger years for thoughts that helped you then. It also shows that a person you work with is immature, be careful what you say around them because they misunderstand things.

Chimney: To see a chimney in the clouds is a sign that you will exceed your expectations. Just stick to the basics. Make sure you use the proper materials or you could fail.

Christ: To see Christ in the clouds points out that you are going through trying times, but with prayer and faith you will come through this. You are being watched over.

Church: To see a church in the clouds reveals that there are people that are willing to help you. All you have to do is ask for the help. You need to seek them out.

Circle: To see a circle in the clouds shows that all you have worked for will be a success. Once you have reached success you have to realize this so you don't go in circles. Also, you need to look inside your family circle, and help those in need.

Clock: To see a clock in the clouds is a sign that you need to hurry. Time is running out. You must use all the available time allotted to you, even if this means you get little sleep.

Clown: To see a clown in the clouds points out that people are tired of your thoughtlessness, and immature actions, you need to grow up. This may be referring to someone close to you.

Coffin: To see a coffin in the clouds reveals that all is not well. You need to get out of your depression or you will have a medical condition that will require hospitalization. You need to get out of your house more and make new friends.

Comb: To see a comb in the clouds shows that you need to get organized, realize who your friends are, and get away from your enemies. It may take some time but if you stick to it you can accomplish this.

Cow: To see a cow in the clouds is a sign that you are happy and content. You have a desire to be left alone. You need to be careful not to be timid or submissive.

Coyote: To see a coyote in the clouds points out that you are surrounded by people who are trying to deceive you. Be wary. You need to insure that someone is not trying to get you to do something illegal.

Crab: To see a crab in the clouds reveals that you need to keep a watchful eye on your business partners or rivals, because they are not what they appear to be. These people can be recognized by their sour temper.

Crane: Seeing a crane in the clouds shows that you are going to have good luck after you help someone in need. The help will include you using machinery.

Crocodile: To see a crocodile in the clouds is a sign that there are people around you that are giving you bad advice. They are jealous of you and are trying to do you harm, even though they seem to be helping you. Be careful for they are out to eat you alive.

Cross: To see a cross in the clouds points out that you are going to suffer, and have grief, but then you shall have good times. Don't give up hope.

Crown: To see a crown in the clouds reveals that you are going to be recognized for your past actions. You will be honored above the rest of the people. Do not let this go to your head.

Crucifix: To see a crucifix in the clouds shows that you will have some hard times to go through, but with faith and prayer you will overcome these problems. Don't lose your faith.

D

The letter D: To see the letter D in the clouds stands for a name of a person, place, or thing.

Deer: To see a deer in the clouds is a sign that you will soon have a friendship that will last a lifetime.

Devil: To see the devil in the clouds points out that you are having problems in your life, and will continue to have problems unless you seek professional help.

Diamond: To see a diamond in the clouds reveals that you are seeking wealth, but will not find what you are looking for. All diamonds are not pure. Some diamonds have many flaws in them that you can't see with the naked eye. Accept what you have.

Dinosaur: To see a dinosaur in the clouds shows that you have been living in the past for too long. It is time to accept new ideas.

Dog: To see a dog in the clouds is a sign that that you will have much pleasure in your social circles. It also means that your friends will be loyal and trustworthy. However, if the dog is snarling, or baring his teeth, you should beware, there is deceit and trickery in store for you.

Dolphins: To see a dolphin in the clouds points out that through your intelligence, you will succeed in the communication field, whether it is at a job or at play.

Donkey: To see a donkey in the clouds reveals that you are going to deal with someone that is very stubborn. You need to have patience in dealing with that person.

Dragon: To see a dragon in the clouds shows that you will be getting financial help from a person of authority. Be careful that person may want back more than you are willing to give.

Drum: To see a drum in the clouds is a sign that you are determined to complete any task your way. Don't walk over someone in the process.

Duck: To see a duck in the clouds points out that you are a very flexible and/ or multi-talented person. You will have good luck in pursuing whatever you want.

E

The letter E: To see the letter E in the clouds stands for a name of a person, place, or thing.

Eagle: To see an eagle in the clouds reveals that you will succeed in your business. This means that you are superior to your fellow workers when it comes to fresh ideas. Let the boss know what you're ideas are. Don't step on people to get the boss to listen to your ideas.

Ear: To see an ear or ears in the clouds shows that you need to pay more attention to what other people are saying. Don't just listen to the words; you'll need to read between the lines to understand what is being said.

Earth: To see the planet earth in the clouds is a sign that you are in tune with the people around you and you have worldly ideas. You will have an opportunity to present your views soon.

Eel: To see an eel in the clouds points out that trouble is headed your way. Don't despair; you will be able to overcome these problems with help from your friends.

Egg: To see an egg in the clouds reveals that you will have good news coming your way. It also means that you need to eat healthier.

Eight: To see the number eight in the clouds is the answer you have been waiting for.

Elephant: To see an elephant in the clouds shows that you will have good luck. It also means that you need to remember your friends and co-workers in their time of need, and give them a helping hand.

Eye: To see an eye in the clouds is a sign that good things are about to happen to you. You need to keep your eyes open to see these good things coming or you will not be able to get the benefits. Use eye protection when needed.

F

The letter F: To see the letter F in the clouds stands for a name of a person, place, or thing.

Face: To see a face in the clouds points out that you will get new friends or coworkers. They will share your moral qualities.

Feet: To see feet in the clouds reveals several things. If you saw big feet, that is a sign that you will soon stabilize your life, and not keep going downhill. If you see small feet this indicates that you should stop and reflect on your past deeds so that you don't make the same mistakes.

Fingers: To see fingers in the clouds shows that you should travel in the direction the finger is pointing. It also means that you will be able to manipulate those around you.

Fish: To see a fish in the clouds is a sign that you need to put God in your life, and put yourself around other God fearing people. Once you do this you will come into some money, and you will get a promotion.

Five: To see the number five in the clouds reveals the answer you have been waiting for.

Four: To see the number four in the clouds points to the answer you have been waiting for.

Fox: To see a fox in the clouds shows that there is danger in the future. It could be a person you are close to, who is clever and resourceful and then conceals that he/she wants to hurt you in some way.

Frog: To see a frog in the clouds is a sign that you have done something that is "unclean", and you need to atone for your actions, and ask for forgiveness.

G

The letter G: To see the letter G in the clouds stands for a name of a person, place, or thing; the color green; the color gold.

Gargoyle: To see a gargoyle in the clouds points out that you have done something that will embarrass you. You are about to be found out. If you fix what "you broke", all will be fine. But do it quickly.

Giraffe: To see a giraffe in the clouds reveals that you are interfering in someone else's affairs. You need to mind your own business. What you are doing might even be considered against the law.

Girl: To see a girl in the clouds shows that you will meet someone who has a playful, childlike nature. Make sure you treat her properly.

Goat: To see a goat in the clouds is a sign that you should refrain from any business venture at this time. You should stay away from gambling. You will get blamed for something you didn't do. Make sure you have a witness around you at all times.

Goldfish: See Fish.

Gorilla: To see a gorilla in the clouds points out that your behavior is gorilla like and because of it you have caused several misunderstandings. You need to explain yourself and clear these up. It also means that there are gangsters that you need to stay away from.

Gravestone: To see a gravestone in the clouds shows that you will be given an opportunity to correct the mistakes that you have made. It also means that someone close to you is gravely ill. Get them to the doctor.

Greyhound: To see a greyhound in the clouds reveals that you will succeed in your venture. You will get more than you expect. The only condition is to stay in the race. Don't give up even if it looks like you are losing.

Gun: To see a gun in the clouds is a sign that someone will do an injustice to you, and you will have to be aggressive in order to get them to correct the injustice. It also means that you are getting ahead of yourself, slow down and watch what you are doing.

H

The letter H: To see the letter H in the clouds stands for a name of a person, place, or thing.

Hammer: To see a hammer in the clouds reveals that you will achieve what you set out to do, but it will require hard work and the right tools, but you will be successful. When you get the opportunity to prove yourself make sure you use all your energy don't hold any back.

Hand: To see a hand in the clouds points out that you will be separated from someone that is dear to you. It is just a temporary goodbye. It also means that someone will lend you a helping hand.

Hare: To see a hare in the clouds shows that there will be a change of work place, or residence. You need to realize that it is for the better. It also means that you will be busy from morning until night.

Hat: To see a hat in the clouds is a sign that you need to conceal something from nosey people. Then you will have good fortune. You can apply for any job that you are qualified for and you will get it.

Head: To see a head in the clouds points out that you will be a leader, or supervisor, but you need to think things out before ordering others around.

Heart: To see a heart in the clouds reveals that you will have favorable results in your love life. You are about to give advice or get advice in matters of the heart.

Horse: To see a horse in the clouds shows that you can handle any situation with ease. You are in control of your emotions. It also means that you need to get better transportation, or a better means to travel.

House: To see a house in the clouds is a sign that you will have financial security. The money gains that you make should be put to good use in your home. It also means that you will have security by investing in a house.

Hummingbird: To see a hummingbird in the clouds points out that your beginnings were small, but if you get busy you will achieve great things. You need to be careful when dealing with fast talking business people.

Hyena: To see a hyena in the clouds reveals that you are surrounded by people that take life as a joke, and are seldom serious. You need to set them straight.

I

The Letter I: The letter I in the clouds stands for a name of a person, place, or thing.

Igloo: To see an Igloo in the clouds is a sign that you need to prepare for the future by insuring you have a place to go to in time of trouble.

Indian: To see an Indian in the clouds shows that you need to go back to your roots. There is something in the past that you need to clear up. Until you clear it up there will be a depression hanging over your head.

Intestine: To see an Intestine in the clouds represents that you will need a lot more information before you can make a good decision. It also means that a medical problem may arise concerning your digestive system.

J

The letter J: To see the Letter J in the clouds stands for a name of a person, place, or thing.

Jeans: To see a pair of Jeans in the clouds reveals that you need to help needy people to insure they have clothing, so they can perform day to day tasks.

Jesus: See Christ.

Jet: To see a jet in the clouds is a sign that you are going to get some bad news from someone who lives far away.

K

The Letter K: To see the letter K in the clouds stands for a name of a person, place, or thing.

Kangaroo: To see a kangaroo in the clouds points out that you will be taking a short trip. You will be required to take charge, and tell others what to do. It also means that you will become very protective of children.

Key: To see a key in the clouds reveals you will find the solution to your problem by yourself. You will need an instrument to help you.

Knife: To see a knife in the clouds shows that you need to explain yourself better and not so aggressively, or you will become separated from someone close to you. It also indicates that the best utensil for the job is a knife.

L

The Letter L: To see the letter L in the clouds means a name a person, place, or thing.

Lamb: To see a lamb in the clouds is a sign that you need to get back to the crowd that has tried to teach you the moral way. If you don't go back to them, you will fall into a crowd that will lead you to your demise. This also indicates that you need not be so timid, and meek.

Light Bulb: To see a light bulb in the clouds shows that you need to shed more light on the subject so that you can solve the problem. It also indicates that you need to be prepared for whatever comes your way.

Lion: To see a lion in the clouds points out that you are meant to be a leader because you possess the qualities of strength and power, and you take pride in your work. It also indicates that other people see you for what your worth and you will profit from this.

Lips: To see lips in the clouds reveals you will have much happiness in love. It also indicates that you should listen and not talk.

Lizard: To see a lizard in the clouds shows that there are close friends of yours who are trying to deceive you. You need to be on your guard. It also indicates that you should stay away from hot, dry cities.

Lobster: To see a lobster in the clouds is a sign that there will be some obstacles in your way, but they are more of a nuisance than a real threat to you. It also means that you need to eat healthier.

Lollipop: To see a lollipop in the clouds points out that you will have happy experiences in the near future. It also points out that you could become a sucker if you are not careful.

M

The letter M: To see the letter M in the clouds stands for a name of a person, place, or thing.

Man: To see a man in the clouds points out that there is a man looking out for you, and the will come to your aid.

Mermaid: To see a mermaid in the clouds reveals you are a dreamer and need to get back to reality. It also indicates that you are in need of a swimming vacation.

Monkey: To see a monkey in the clouds is a sign that you need to quit playing around so much and acting immature, or you will lose your friends.

Moose: To see a moose in the clouds points out that there is a change in your life coming. It suggests that an older person may be involved. It also shows that this person is a very large adult male.

Motorcycle: To see a motorcycle in the clouds reveals your need to be left alone so that you can think more clearly. It also indicates that you need to be very careful around motorcycles.

Mouse: To see a mouse in the clouds shows that you will have problems from friends and family but these will be overcome. So don't be in despair about these problems. It also shows that you may be involved in an altercation, and you may get a mouse(black eye), under your eye.

N

The letter N: To see the Letter N in the clouds stands for a name of a person, place, or thing.

Nine: To see the number nine in the clouds is the answer you have been waiting for.

Nuts: To see nuts in the clouds reveals that you have an impulse to do something crazy. You need to act mature and not give in to your impulses. It also reveals that you need to eat more nuts.

O

The Letter O: To see the letter O in the clouds stands for a name of a person, place, or thing; the color orange.

Octopus: To see an octopus in the clouds shows that there is too much going on in your life. You need to let someone else handle some of the tasks that you are doing. It also reveals that there is a powerful organization that you need to beware of.

One: If you see the number one in the clouds, this is the answer you have been looking for.

Ostrich: To see an ostrich in the clouds points out that you are afraid to face the future. You have buried your head in the ground. You need to get some help, and then you will be able to face any situation that comes your way. It also reveals that you have items that are useless. You need to discard them, or they will weigh you down.

Otter: To see an otter in the clouds reveals that the time has come for you to put away for a rainy day or you will be left with serious financial problems. It also reveals that you are due for a swimming vacation.

Ox: To see an ox in the clouds shows that in order for to you to gain wealth, you have to do much work.

Oyster: To see an oyster in the clouds is a sign that you need to be careful who you trust. Check them out carefully before you open up to them. You also need to re-look at all the items you have been saving over the years, you may find that they contain wealth you were unaware of.

Owl: To see an Owl in the clouds point out that you are surrounded by people who have wisdom, but be careful because they don't have your best interest in mind. These people are experts at getting close to you undetected.

P

The letter P: To see the letter P in the clouds stands for a name of a person, place, or thing; the color purple or pink.

Panda Bear: To see a Panda Bear in the clouds reveals that you need to find a common ground in dealing with other people.

Peacock: To see a peacock in the clouds shows that you are spending too much time making yourself look beautiful. You need to get down to earth and realize beauty is only skin deep. You are a vain person.

Pelican: To see a pelican in the clouds points out that others have a need for your nurturing. You need to help them. It also points out that you need to save for a rainy day.

Penguin: To see a penguin in the clouds reveals your problems will melt away because they aren't as serious as you thought they were. This also indicates that you need to take a swimming vacation.

Pig: To see a pig in the clouds shows that you need to beware of greed, and selfishness that are headed your way. You need to be careful and not fall into a trap. This also indicates that you need to go on a diet.

Pony: To see a pony in the clouds is a sign that someone close to you needs your guidance more than ever. It also shows that you need to pay your debts on time.

Popcorn: To see popcorn in the clouds point out that your health will remain good if you take care of yourself with regular check-ups. It also shows that you need to enjoy the little things in life, and you don't need to spend a lot of money to have a good time.

Pretzel: To see a pretzel in the clouds reveals that something is confusing you, but you will be able to unscramble the puzzle and solve the problem. It also shows that you need to watch your salt intake and not eat so many salted products.

Puppy: To see a puppy in the clouds shows your ability to get along with anyone. You will have many friends if you continue in this manner. It also shows that you need to stay away from conceited people, or their actions will turn you into a conceited person.

Pyramid: To see a pyramid in the clouds is a sign that you are well established in your community. To continue without any problems you need to continue doing the things that got you where you are now. It also shows that you need to beware of salesmen who have an offer that sounds too good to be true. They will try to get your money, and give you nothing in return.

Q

The Letter Q: To see the letter Q in the clouds stands for a name of a person, place, or thing.

    Quilt: See Blanket.

R

The letter R: To see the letter R in the clouds stands for a name of a person, place, or thing; the color red.

Rabbit: To see a rabbit in the clouds points out that you will continue to have good luck, so you need to take advantage of this. It also indicates that in time of trouble sometimes it is better to flee than to fight, especially when you are out-numbered.

Raccoon: To see a raccoon in the clouds reveals that you need to beware of friends of yours who are conniving against you and that are jealous of you so they are spreading lies about you. It also indicates that these "friends" of yours like to stay out all night and party.

Ram: To see a ram in the clouds shows that you are being pushed around by someone, or several people. You need to stand up for yourself. It also shows that you need to arm yourself to be prepared for an attack.

Rat: To see a rat in the clouds is a sign that there are certain people in your group that are jealous of you and are going to try to get you in trouble. These people will betray your cause.

Reindeer: To see a reindeer in the clouds points out that you are going to come into financial gain. You have something of value, but you don't know the value. You need to find out the value.

Reptile: To see a reptile in the clouds reveals that you will encounter a low-life. You will recognize this person by his immaturity, and lack of a job. He will give you complements, and tell you about a hard time he has had. Don't fall for his flattery.

Rhinoceros: To see a rhinoceros in the clouds shows that you need to be more assertive and you have to be careful to meet all you're obligations, or there will be severe consequences. This also indicates that you need to go on a diet.

Rifle: See Gun.

Ring: See Circle.

Rooster: To see a rooster in the clouds is a sign that you have been showing off a little too much lately. You need to get out of the spotlight and let someone else enjoy the spotlight.

S

The letter S: To see the letter S in the clouds stands for a name of a person, place, or thing; the color silver.

Sailboat: To see a sailboat in the clouds points out that you want to be the one in charge. Once you take charge there will be clear sailing.

Seal: To see a seal in the clouds reveals that you are a fortunate person. You will prosper in love and in business. You have the ability to separate your business from pleasure. You will have many reliable friends.

Serpent: See Snake.

Seven: The number seven in the clouds is the answer to the question you have been waiting for.

Shark: To see a shark in the clouds points out a warning about your friend and/or associates. They are a dishonest lot. You need to separate the lies from the truth. Don't take their word for anything. You need to verify what they tell you before you use their information.

Sheep: To see sheep in the clouds reveals that you are not looking before you leap. You are only following the crowd. Branch out on your own and don't follow the crowd to your demise.

Six: To see the number six in the clouds is the answer to your question.

Skull: To see a skull in the clouds shows a warning. There is danger and/or death in your future. It could be a stranger, or someone you know. Keep a careful eye out and this may be prevented.

Skunk: To see a skunk in the clouds is a sign that people are avoiding you. You need to ask why so that you can correct this problem. Once you make a change all will be well.

Snake: To see a snake in the clouds points out that certain people are out to do you harm. You need to be aware of this so you can protect yourself.

Spider: To see a spider in the clouds reveals that you will be tempted to do something that you should not do. Don't be tempted.

Squirrel: To see a squirrel in the clouds shows that you need to change direction in your personal and business direction. Once you do, you will get benefits.

Stars: To see a star in the clouds is a sign that you will succeed beyond your wildest dreams.

Swing: To see a swing in the clouds points out that you will find a solution to your problem by remembering your childhood, and taking an experience that you had then and using the solution to solve your problem now.

T

The letter T: To see the letter T in the clouds stands for a name a person, place, or thing.

Table: To see a table in the clouds reveals that you will prosper in the years to come, and have many family gatherings, and/or meetings at your business that you will profit from.

Ten: Seeing the number ten in the clouds is the answer to your question.

Tent: To see a tent in the clouds shows that all your worries will go away once you take a vacation, and get some rest. You have been working yourself too hard.

Three: Seeing the number three in the clouds is the answer to your question.

Tortoise: To see a tortoise in the clouds is a sign that you have not been living up to your potential. You need to make a few changes and you will be successful.

Tree: To see a tree in the clouds points out that you will realize all your desires. You have planted a seed and watched it mature. You will have a lasting success.

Truck: To see a truck in the clouds shows that you will make it to the top, and can ride now.

Turkey: To see a turkey in the clouds reveals that you have a reunion of sorts, but you will be roasted and made fun of.

Turtle: To see a turtle in the clouds shows that you are on the right track, however, you are moving too slowly. Others will get there first and leave you without anything.

Two: Seeing the number two in the clouds is the answer to your question.

U

The letter U: To see the letter U in the clouds stands for a name of a person, place, or thing.

Umbrella: To see an umbrella in the clouds is a sign that you will have job security, and you have prepared for the future.

Unicorn: To see a unicorn in the clouds points out that there will be changes in your life that are beneficial to you.

V

The letter V: To see the letter V in the clouds stands for a name of a person, place, or thing.

Vehicle: See car, truck, motorcycle.

Virgin Mary: To see the Virgin Mary in the clouds reveals that you are being watched after, and whatever you prayed for will be answered soon, and to your benefit.

W

The letter W: To see the letter W in the clouds stands for a name of a person, place, or thing. It could also stand for the color white.

Wagon: To see a wagon in the clouds shows that there will be difficult time ahead for you. This also indicates that someone is out for revenge against you, and you need to beware.

Walrus: To see a walrus in the clouds is a sign that you will become the dominant partner in your relationship.

Whale: To see a whale in the clouds points out that you will be able to handle any task given to you to do, with the help of your friends. With your ability and their help you will succeed.

Witch: To see a witch in the clouds is a warning that you have people in your circle that are jealous of you, and are trying to harm you.

Wolf: To see a wolf in the clouds is a sign that there will be hard times ahead, and there are people who want your job. You must stick to yourself, and count on your instincts to survive.

Wrench: To see a wrench in the clouds indicates that you are going to have mechanical problems if you don't do preventive maintenance on your vehicle.

X

The letter X: To see the letter X in the clouds stands for a name of a person, place, or thing.

Xylophone: To see a xylophone in the clouds reveals that you or someone close to you will do well with any musical instrument.

Y

The letter Y: To see the letter Y in the clouds stands for a name of a person, place, or thing. It could also stand for the color yellow.

Z

The letter Z: To see the letter Z in the clouds stands for a name of a person, place, or thing.

Zebra: To see a zebra in the clouds shows that the things that you have done up to this point are correct and balanced. Continue on this path or risk ridicule and failure.

Endnotes

1. Salinas, David. Interviewed by Franklin A. Tyler Jr. June 15 2007. San Antonio, Texas.

2. Luke 11:1 The World English Bible (WEB) [updated October 3 2007; cited November 27 2007] Available from http://eBible.org/web/

3. Matthew 6:9-13 The World English Bible (WEB) [updated October 3 2007; cited November 27 2007] Available from http://eBible.org/web/

4. Luke 11:2-4 The World English Bible (WEB) [updated October 3 2007; cited November 27 2007] Available from http://eBible.org/web/

5. 2 Chronicles 7-14 The World English Bible (WEB) [updated October 3 2007; cited November 27 2007] Available from http://eBible.org/web/

6. Matthew 6:5-8 The World English Bible (WEB) [updated October 3 2007; cited November 27 2007] Available from http://eBible.org/web/

7. Luke 11:9-13 The World English Bible (WEB) [updated October 3 2007; cited November 27 2007] Available from http://eBible.org/web/

8. Genesis 1:3 The World English Bible (WEB) [updated October 3 2007; cited November 27 2007] Available from http://eBible.org/web/

9. Genesis 1:6 The World English Bible (WEB) [updated October 3 2007; cited November 27 2007] Available from http://eBible.org/web/

10. Genesis 1:28 The World English Bible (WEB) [updated October 3 2007; cited November 27 2007] Available from http://eBible.org/web/

11. Genesis 15:1 The World English Bible (WEB) [updated October 3 2007; cited November 27 2007] Available from http://eBible.org/web/

12. Genesis 15:2 The World English Bible (WEB) [updated October 3 2007; cited November 27 2007] Available from http://eBible.org/web/

13. Numbers 12:5-6 The World English Bible (WEB) [updated October 3 2007; cited November 27 2007] Available from http://eBible.org/web/

14. Genesis 28:12-16 The World English Bible (WEB) [updated October 3 2007; cited November 27 2007] Available from http://eBible.org/web/

15. Exodus 24:12 The World English Bible (WEB) [updated October 3 2007; cited November 27 2007] Available from http://eBible.org/web/

16. Exodus 31:18 The World English Bible (WEB) [updated October 3 2007; cited November 27 2007] Available from http://eBible.org/web/

17. Deuteronomy 9:10 The World English Bible (WEB) [updated October 3 2007; cited November 27 2007] Available from http://eBible.org/web/

18. Daniel 5:1 The World English Bible (WEB) [updated October 3 2007; cited November 27 2007] Available from http://eBible.org/web/

19. Daniel 5:5 The World English Bible (WEB) [updated October 3 2007; cited November 27 2007] Available from http://eBible.org/web/

20. Daniel 5:25 The World English Bible (WEB) [updated October 3 2007; cited November 27 2007] Available from http://eBible.org/web/

21. Daniel 5:26 The World English Bible (WEB) [updated October 3 2007; cited November 27 2007] Available from http://eBible.org/web/

22. Daniel 5:27 The World English Bible (WEB) [updated October 3 2007; cited November 27 2007] Available from http://eBible.org/web/

23. Daniel 5:28 The World English Bible (WEB) [updated October 3 2007; cited November 27 2007] Available from http://eBible.org/web/

24. Daniel 5:30 The World English Bible (WEB) [updated October 3 2007; cited November 27 2007] Available from http://eBible.org/web/

25. Exodus 13:21-22 The World English Bible (WEB) [updated October 3 2007; cited November 27 2007] Available from http://eBible.org/web/

26. Exodus 16:10 The World English Bible (WEB) [updated October 3 2007; cited November 27 2007] Available from http://eBible.org/web/

27. Exodus 19:9 The World English Bible (WEB) [updated October 3 2007; cited November 27 2007] Available from http://eBible.org/web/

28. Numbers 11:25 The World English Bible (WEB) [updated October 3 2007; cited November 27 2007] Available from http://eBible.org/web/

29. Isaiah 19:1 The World English Bible (WEB) [updated October 3 2007; cited November 27 2007] Available from http://eBible.org/web/

30. Matthew 17:5 The World English Bible (WEB) [updated October 3 2007; cited November 27 2007] Available from http://eBible.org/web/

31. Genesis 1:1 The World English Bible (WEB) [updated October 3 2007; cited November 27 2007] Available from http://eBible.org/web/

32. Genesis 1:14-18 The World English Bible (WEB) [updated October 3 2007; cited November 27 2007] Available from http://eBible.org/web/

33. Deuteronomy 4:39 The World English Bible (WEB) [updated October 3 2007; cited November 27 2007] Available from http://eBible.org/web/

34. Deuteronomy 26:15 The World English Bible (WEB) [updated October 3 2007; cited November 27 2007] Available from http://eBible.org/web/

35. Psalms 33:13 The World English Bible (WEB) [updated October 3 2007; cited November 27 2007] Available from http://eBible.org/web/

36. Psalms 102:19 The World English Bible (WEB) [updated October 3 2007; cited November 27 2007] Available from http://eBible.org/web/

37. Psalms 147:8 The World English Bible (WEB) [updated October 3 2007; cited November 27 2007] Available from http://eBible.org/web/

38. Mark 11:25 The World English Bible (WEB) [updated October 3 2007; cited November 27 2007] Available from http://eBible.org/web/

39. Mark 14:62 The World English Bible (WEB) [updated October 3 2007; cited November 27 2007] Available from http://eBible.org/web/

40. John 6:38 The World English Bible (WEB) [updated October 3 2007; cited November 27 2007] Available from http://eBible.org/web/

41. Deuteronomy 18:9-12 The World English Bible (WEB) [updated October 3 2007; cited November 27 2007] Available from http://eBible.org/web/

References of some of the people I interviewed

Acosta, Freddy. Interviewed by Franklin A. Tyler Jr. 1996, 1997, 1998, 1999 San Antonio, Texas.

Applegate, John. Interviewed by Franklin A. Tyler Jr. 1982, 1983 Fort Riley Kansas.

Alba, Hope. Interviewed by Franklin A. Tyler Jr. 1982, 1983, 1984, 1985, 1986, 1987, 1990, 1990, 1991,1992 San Antonio, Texas.

Borrego, Dora. Interviewed by Franklin A. Tyler Jr. 1982, 1983, 1984, 1985, 1986, 1987, 1990, 1991, 1992 San Antonio, Texas.

Dubois, Jacques. Interviewed by Franklin A. Tyler Jr.1990 Paris, France

Garcia, Andrew. Interviewed by Franklin A. Tyler Jr. 1992 Cotulla, Texas.

Garcia, Jesus. Interviewed by Franklin A. Tyler Jr. 1993, 1994, 1995 Hondo, Texas.

Moretti, Carlo. Interviewed by Franklin A. Tyler Jr. 1990 Genoa, Italy.

Probst, Resti. Interviewed by Franklin A. Tyler Jr. 1990 Zurich, Switzerland.

Sablan, Margret. Interviewed by Franklin A. Tyler Jr. 1984, 1985, 1986, Fort Leonard wood Missouri. 1992 Tacoma, Washington.

Rivera, Luis. Interviewed by Franklin A. Tyler Jr. 2000, 2001, 2002, 2003, 2004, 2005, 2006, 2007 San Antonio Texas

Salinas, David. Interviewed by Franklin A. Tyler Jr. 2000, 2001, 2002, 2003, 2004, 2005, 2006, 2007 San Antonio, Texas

Schneider, Fritz. Interviewed by Franklin A. Tyler Jr. 1988, 1989,1990 Frankfurt, Germany.

The World English Bible (WEB) [updated October 3 2007; cited November 27 2007] Available from http://eBible.org/web/

978-0-595-47938-2
0-595-47938-3

www.ingramcontent.com/pod-product-compliance
Lightning Source LLC
Chambersburg PA
CBHW020400290526
45785CB00005B/2382